The Church Next Door

Written by: Scott Pugh
Illustrated by: Miguel Hernandez
© 2015

Dedicated to my children, Madeline and Owen, for understanding why it's so important to tell everyone about God's love.

NOTE TO PARENTS: Jamie Reese is a good friend of mine who is a children's director at a church in Massillon, Ohio. One of the reasons I think so much of Jamie is because she truly loves children. She cheers for them, hopes for them, dreams with them, and spends countless hours defending how important they really are. One of her constant phrases is, "When kids accept Jesus as their savior, they don't get a miniature version of the Holy Spirit." Jamie is right!

As you flip through the pages of scripture you will find that Jesus said the most amazing things about young people. He said things like, "Don't look down on them." "Don't cause them to stumble." My personal favorite was when Jesus said that children were the greatest in the kingdom of heaven….and that's why I wrote this book. I wrote this to help the children of church planters and children all across the world understand how important and influential they really are. Children don't have a miniature version of God's love, power, or grace. They are capable, even at a young age, to help others learn what it means to follow Jesus.

As you read through this book with your children, there are several key questions that you can discuss as a family.

1. Why is starting a new church so important?

2. Is there someone in your school, on your baseball team, or dance class that you could invite to church?

3. Why is it so important to make new kids feel welcome at church on Sunday morning?

As you embark on your church-planting journey, I hope that hundreds and thousands of people will discover who Jesus really is and how to follow him on a daily basis. I also hope that your children (and the children of your new congregation) are discipled to be the people God created them to be.

Hi. My name is Briana. I am 10 years old and I want to tell you a story about something that happened to me this summer and how my whole life changed.

I live with my mom and my brother Javan in a big city called Hudson. We live right next door to Sunview Elementary School, which is where I go to school.

I like living next to my school because during the summer, and in the evening, there is a lot of room to play. My brother and I ride our bikes in the big school parking lot. All of the neighborhood kids come and play kickball in the field, but the best part of living next to my school is that I can go to the playground any time I want.

One Sunday, just before school started, Javan and I were pretending to be racecar drivers. We were pedaling our bikes as fast as we could from one end of the school parking lot to the other. We made several laps around the black top when a few cars pulled into the school. I wasn't sure why they were there, because it was Sunday, and no one ever comes to the school on Sunday.

I stood at a distance and watched as people got out of their cars and walked into the school. They were carrying boxes, bags, chairs, and one guy even had a guitar. I wondered what they were doing so I walked over to see. As I got a little closer I saw a girl who looked my age. When she saw me, she waved her hand and shouted, "Hi."

I didn't have black pants or a black shirt, but I remembered watching a movie where a man was a spy and he wore a long brown coat. So I went to the closet, put on my mom's tan raincoat, looked in the mirror, and thought, "This will do just fine."

Javan and I ran out the front door to start our investigation. We tiptoed across the parking lot and hid behind a tree in front of the school. Just a few seconds later, Javan and I saw something we couldn't believe! Hundreds of people drove their cars into the school parking lot. The cars were filled with families from all over Hudson. There were adults, teenagers, and even kids who went to my school. One by one they all began to file into the school.

Javan and I were shocked. We had no idea what was going on. We stayed hidden behind the big tree with our bodies low to the ground in order to keep from being seen. Every few seconds we would tilt our heads and lean to the side just far enough that our eyes could see past the big tree trunk we were hiding behind.

Then we heard the most unusual sound. We heard the sound of children singing, clapping, and laughing. It was one of the most magical sounds I had ever heard. Javan and I didn't know where the sounds were coming from so we decided to take a closer look.

We made a plan to sneak from the tree to the bushes that were next to the school. We crouched down as low as we could so that no one could see us and carefully made our way to the bushes outside of the classroom windows.

When we made it to the bushes, we raised our heads up just enough to peek in the window and we were amazed at what we saw. There was a man with a guitar singing songs with about 30 or 40 children. All the kids were singing and clapping along with the music. It looked like so much fun!

As I stood there watching all these kids I started to wonder, "What are they singing about? Where did they learn these songs and why are all these kids here on Sunday?" I had all kinds of thoughts racing through my mind so I turned to Javan and said, "Let's find out what else is going on here."

Using our best secret agent moves, we snuck around to the back of the building and hid behind a big rock. Then we crawled from the big rock to the shrubs that were next to the gym. We felt like real secret agents because no one saw us.

When we got to the shrubs we heard someone talking in the gym. So we bent down and slowly made our way to the playground. We climbed up the monkey bars so that we could look inside the gym. As we peered through the window, we saw that the stage had a beautiful background and lights were set up all around the room.

The gym floor was filled with people sitting on chairs and we saw a man on the stage talking, but we couldn't hear what he was saying. Javan and I sat on top of the monkey bars and watched the man on the stage for several minutes. Then Javan said, "What do you think he's saying?"

"I don't know," I answered. "I've never seen anything like this before."

Just then the people in the gym stood up and began to leave. Javan and I jumped off the monkey bars and ran to the parking lot to see what was going to happen next. Moments later, all the people who were inside the school came out, got in their cars, and began to leave.

We squatted down beside a picnic table and Javan took out his binoculars. He put them up to his face so he could get a closer look at the people leaving our school. As my brother was looking through the binoculars he pointed and said, "Hey, there's Mike from my baseball team! I see Stacey from your dance class! And there's Mr. Holland our principal!"

A few minutes later we saw a young girl walk out of the school. I couldn't recognize who she was because we were too far away, so I asked Javan to use his binoculars. He handed them to me and as I looked through the lenses I noticed that it was the same girl who waved at me earlier that morning. She looked like she was the same age as me, but I had never seen her before.

I turned to my brother and said, "Javan, I'm going to go and talk with her to find out what was going on at the school this morning."

"Okay," Javan said. "I'll go with you."

We hopped up from behind the picnic table and started walking towards the girl. She was standing near a car in the parking lot. As we got closer I said, "Hi. My name is Briana and this is my brother Javan. We live in the house next door."

"Hi," the little girl said. "My name is Madeline. It's nice to meet you."

"It's nice to meet you too," I said. "We were playing secret agents today and we saw all the people going into the school. Why was everyone here on a Sunday?"

Madeline said, "Well, my family moved to Hudson this summer to start a new church and we meet here on Sunday mornings."

"Your church meets at our school?" I asked. "I thought all churches met in church buildings."

Madeline smiled at me and said, "I used to think that too. My dad is a pastor and he told me that when churches first get started, they don't have a building, so they meet wherever they can. Some new churches meet at the mall. Some new churches meet in movie theaters and some new churches meet in school buildings."

"There are churches that meet in movie theaters?" I asked. "Do they give you popcorn?"

Madeline laughed and said, "I don't know. I've never been to a church that meets in a movie theater. I've only heard about them from my dad, but my new church is really great. Why don't both of you come with me next week and you can see it for yourself."

"Okay," I said. "That sounds like fun."

The next Sunday, Javan and I met Madeline in the school parking lot. We weren't sure what to expect because we'd never been to a church before. When we walked into the building there were at least five people who said hello to us. They shook our hand, asked us our names, what grade we were in, and one man even asked me what my favorite movie was. I told him it was Cinderella.

Next we followed Madeline around the corner and saw something amazing. This church had a table that was stacked with donuts, cookies, fruit, coffee, and juice boxes. I looked at Madeline and asked, "Who are all those donuts and cookies for?"

"They are for us," Madeline said. "We put donuts and cookies on that table every week just for kids."

"Are you kidding?" I asked.

Madeline smiled and said, "Nope. I'm not kidding at all. It's just one of the ways that our church tries to show kids how much they matter."

I walked over to the table, picked out a big chocolate chip cookie and a grape juice box. My brother Javan got a donut and we followed Madeline down the hallway toward the classrooms. As we walked down the hall I heard music and laughter coming from one of the rooms.

When we walked through the door I saw a lot of kids from my school. They were playing games, jumping rope, and having a good time.

As soon as we walked in the room, three adults came over and introduced themselves to us. One lady said, "Hi my name is Rose. What's your name?"

"My name is Briana and this is my brother Javan," I said.

"Well it's nice to meet both of you," Rose said. "Is this your first time here?"

I nodded my head and replied, "I go to school here, but it's my first time at church."

"Well I'm so glad you came today," Rose said. "You're going to have a great time."

A few minutes later the adults told us that it was time to get things started, so all the kids gathered in the middle of the room. We sang three really fun songs, danced around the room, and clapped along with the music.

Then Rose got up in the front of the room and she told us a story about a man named Jesus. I had never heard a story about Jesus before and this one was really good.

It was about how a little boy had five loaves of bread, two fish, and gave them to Jesus. Then Jesus took that little bit of food and fed over 5,000 people.

When the service was over Javan and I went home. We told our mom about all the fun we had and how people were so nice to us. We told her about the cookies, donuts, juice boxes, and the music. We even told her the story of how Jesus fed 5,000 people with just five pieces of bread and a couple fish. My mom was happy that we had a good time at church. She even said that she would go with us the very next week.

That next Sunday my whole family went to church. As soon as we walked in people greeted me with high fives. It was almost like they were excited to see me. They said, "Hey Briana! How are you? Did you watch Cinderella this week?" I couldn't believe they remembered my name and that my favorite movie was Cinderella.

Madeline met Javan and I in the hallway and we walked to class together. As soon as I walked into the room Rose hugged me and said, "I'm so glad you came back. It's great to see you again Briana." Seeing Rose made me smile. I felt like she really cared about me and that she was happy that I was there. It made me feel special.

That morning we laughed and prayed. We learned more about Jesus and I left the school feeling happier and more loved than I ever had before.

As I laid in bed that night I started thinking something that I've never thought about before. I wondered what the world would be like if every child had a church.

I thought, "What would happen if every child across the world went to a church like the one next door? A place that was filled with smiles, music, and laughter. What would it be like if every kid had a church where adults knew their name, their favorite movie, and gave them hugs and high fives when they walked in the door? What if every child had a church?

What would happen if donuts and cookies were given to kids just to show them that they matter? What if the sound of drums and guitars made every young person smile the way it made me smile? What if every child learned more about Jesus and all the things he did for people?"

As I faded off to sleep that night I really believed that the world would be a different place…..if every child had a church.

The Church Next Door

Written by: Scott Pugh
scott@velocitycleveland.org

Illustrated by: Miguel Hernandez
Penhitsthepad.com

Cover Design by: Jason Maric
facebook.com/JasonMaricArt

ISBN: 978-1-4951-0554-8

Copyright © 2015 by Scott Pugh

All rights reserved. No part of this book may be reproduced or transmitted in any form or by any mean, electronic or mechanical, including photocopying and recording, or any information storage and retrieval system, without permission in writing from author and illustrator.

Other books by Scott Pugh

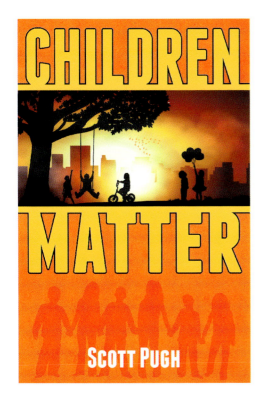

ISLAM IN THE HINTERLANDS